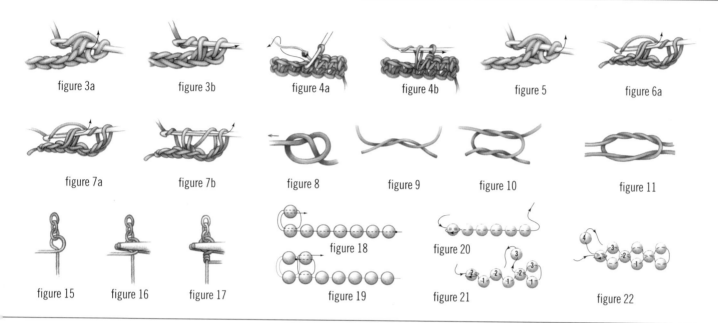

figure 3a   figure 3b   figure 4a   figure 4b   figure 5   figure 6a

figure 7a   figure 7b   figure 8   figure 9   figure 10   figure 11

figure 15   figure 16   figure 17   figure 18   figure 20   figure 22

figure 19   figure 21

stitch from the hook, yarn over, and draw through the stitch (3 loops on the hook). **Figure 6b:** Yarn over and draw through 2 loops on the hook (2 loops on the hook). **Figure 6c:** Yarn over and draw through the remaining 2 loops on the hook (1 loop remains).

half-double crochet: Figure 7a: Yarn over. Insert the hook through the first or second stitch from the hook, yarn over, and draw through the stitch (3 loops on the hook). **Figure 7b:** Yarn over and draw through all 3 loops on the hook (1 loop on the hook).

overhand knot: Figure 8: Make a loop in the cord and bring the end that crosses on top behind the loop. Then pull it through to the front.

square knot: Figure 9: Bring the left-hand cord over the right-hand cord and around. **Figure 10:** Cross right over left and go through the loop.

surgeon's knot: The extra wrap makes the top curl around the sides for a stronger knot. **Figure 11:** Begin as a square knot: **figures 9** and **10**). Go through the loop again, then tighten.

wrapped loops: Figure 12: Leaving a 1-in. (2.5cm) tail, place the tip of a chainnose pliers against where the bead will be. Bend the tail to form a right angle.
Figure 13: With roundnose pliers, grasp the tail just past the bend and pull it over the jaw to point the other way.
Figure 14: Loosen the pliers grip enough to rotate them so the empty jaw is above the partial loop and continue pulling the tail around the bottom jaw until it's perpendicular to the wire.
Figure 15: Pull a split ring, chain, etc., into the loop. **Figure 16:** To keep the loop round, grasp it with roundnose pliers in your non-dominant hand above the cross. Wrap the pliers' jaws with masking tape to avoid denting the wire. **Figure 17:** Grasp the tail with chainnose pliers to pull it around the wire until it meets the bead. Make the first wrap against the pliers; keep wraps close together. One wrap will keep the loop from opening; additional wraps are decorative. Clip. Press the cut end in with chainnose pliers.

square stitch: Figure 18: String the required number of beads for the first row. Then string the first bead of the second row and go through the last

bead of the first row and the first bead of the second row in the same direction. The new bead sits on top of the old bead and the holes are horizontal. **Figure 19:** String the second bead of row 2 and go through the next-to-last bead of row 1. Continue through the new bead of row 2. Repeat this step for the entire row.

even-count flat peyote: Figure 20: String one bead and loop through it again in the same direction, leaving a 3-4-in. (8-10cm) tail. String beads to total an even number. These beads comprise the first two rows. (Remove the extra loop and weave the tail into the work after a few rows.) **Figure 21:** Every other bead from **figure 20** drops down half a space to form row 1. To begin row 3 (count rows diagonally), pick up a bead and stitch through the second bead from the end. Pick up a bead and go through the fourth bead from the end. Continue in this manner. End by going through the first bead strung. **Figure 22:** To start row 4 and all other rows, pick up a bead and go through the last bead added on the previous row.

Weave through the work in a zigzag path to end thread. Begin a thread the same way, exiting the last bead added in the same direction to resume.

Easy crochet bracelet

This very easy chain-stitch crochet bracelet works up in a jiffy with size 8º seed beads. Once you master the technique with large seed beads, make a dainty version with size 11º beads. Use a coordinating shank button as a clasp. A wristful of these simple bracelets looks great.

crochet the bracelet

❶ Thread a needle onto the end of a spool of Nymo D. Do not cut the thread from the spool.

❷ String a 3¼-in. (8cm) pattern, mixing 8º seed beads, 2-3 triangle beads, and a crystal (**photo a**). Repeat your pattern 6 times, then end with another 3¼ in. of seed and triangle beads. This length of strung beads makes a 7½-in.-long (19cm) bracelet.

❸ Remove the needle from the thread and use a crochet hook to make a chain stitch (see "Basics," p. 3), leaving a 14-in. (36cm) tail.

❹ Slide 3 beads against the hook and make a beaded chain stitch (see "Basics" and **photo b**). Continue making 3-bead chain stitches (**photo c**) until you reach the first crystal. The last stitch before the crystal could have either 2 or 4 beads.

❺ Secure your work before the crystal by enlarging the last loop and passing the worked section through it (**photo d**). Then tighten the loop next to the last chain stitch. Slide the crystal up to the worked section. Make a loop after the crystal as for an overhand knot (see "Basics") and pass the worked section through it (**photo e**). Slip the crochet hook into the loop before tightening.

❻ Repeat steps 4-5 until you have crocheted the entire strand. Cut the thread from the spool, leaving a 20-in. (51cm) tail and pull the tail through the last loop to secure the chain.

finishing

❶ Thread a needle on the ending tail. String an 8º or a crystal, 1-2 seed beads, the button, and 1-2 seed beads. Sew back through the crystal or 8º and 1-2 beads on the

materials

- **350** Seed beads, size 8º
- **20-30** Accent beads: triangle beads, tiny teardrops, etc.
- **8** 5-6mm Bicone or Czech fire-polished crystals
- **1g** Seed beads, size 11º
- **1** Spool Nymo D
- **1** ½-in. (1.3cm) Shank button
- Beading needles, #12
- G-S Hypo Cement
- Steel crochet hook, size 11

last chain stitch (**photo f**). Repeat the thread path twice for security.

❷ Sew back through the the bracelet in a straight line, passing through 1-2 of the beads in each chain stitch and every crystal. When you reach the other end, string an 8º or a crystal and test the length of the bracelet. If it's too long, gather up the length slightly.

❸ String enough 11º seed beads to make a loop that fits over the button and sew back through the crystal or 8º (**photo g**). Tie the working thread to the thread tail at the starting end with a surgeon's knot (see "Basics"). Glue the knot.

❹ Reinforce the loop and tie another surgeon's knot with the tails. Sew through a few more beads with each tail before trimming the thread. ⦿
— *Diane Dow*

Creative bead crochet

Bead crochet ropes make beautiful and stylish necklaces and bracelets. They're gorgeous in monochromatic color schemes but they can also be created in just about any pattern you desire.

For your first project, use larger beads strung in a stripe pattern—one white, one black, for example. That way you'll always know which bead is next.

After you've mastered the basic techniques (see p. 18), use the following procedure to create your own patterns.

Simply crochet 1-2 inches in plain white beads. Draw your pattern (diamonds, hearts, letters, etc.) onto the bead rope with permanent colored markers (**photo a**). Then unravel the rope (**photo b**). Now you have the correct stringing order for the entire pattern on your thread (**photo c**). You can bead whole stories on a rope or use subtle shades to fade a rainbow across a piece. ⦿ — *LynneMarie Creed*

a

b

c

Fast and fabulous

In the commercial fishing harbors near my home in *Hawai'i*, fishermen work with nets covered in sparkling drops of water. These necklaces—with their crystals, pearls, and gemstones held captive by wire—remind me of those glistening fishing nets.

The necklaces work up quickly and are fun to make. In no time at all, you can add a high-fashion accessory to your jewelry collection.

Be prepared to attract some attention, however. Strangers are bound to stop you to admire your handiwork.

With a crochet wire necklace, lightness is essential; add a heavy bead and it will droop. The finer the wire, the lighter and more flexible the necklace. You can use fine-gauge sterling, gold-filled, and copper wire as well as Artistic Wire, which is available in many colors.

For a choker-style necklace, keep all the strands the same length. For a graduated drape, cut each strand a few inches longer than the previous one. Working with crochet hooks of different sizes changes the length of chain you make from a given length of wire. Changing the wire gauge affects both loop size and strand length.

crocheted strands

❶ To determine the length of the crocheted strands, subtract the length of the cones and clasp from the desired length of your finished necklace. For strands approximately 14-in. (35cm) long, cut six 6-ft. (1.8m) lengths of wire.

❷ Starting about 2 in. (5cm) from one end of a wire strand, make 3 chain stitches (see "Basics," p. 3) with loops large enough to accommodate the crochet hook, but not much larger (**photo a**). Keep the tension and loop size even as you work.

❸ String a bead on the long tail of wire and push it close to the last chain stitch. Catch the wire above the bead with the hook and pull it through the loop to make another chain stitch, but don't pull the bead through the loop (**photo b**). Make another 3 chain stitches.

❹ Repeat step 3, stringing a random mix of pearls and other beads, until you have about 2 in. of wire left. (You can enhance the necklace's airy, freeform look by varying the number of chain stitches between beads.) When you've made the last chain stitch, pull the wire tail through the loop.

❺ Crochet 5 more strands to complete the necklace. As you work, vary the bead placement to give the finished piece a

---

materials

- 36 ft. (11m) 28- or 30-gauge Wire
- Pearls, assorted colors and sizes
- Crystals and/or glass beads, assorted colors and sizes
- 2 Head pins or 6 in. (15cm) 22-gauge wire
- 2 1-in. (2.5cm) Cones
- Clasp or 1 ft. (30cm) 18-gauge wire
- Size J or K crochet hook

Tools: round- and chainnose pliers, diagonal wire cutters, hammer (optional)

---

pleasing distribution of colors, shapes, and sizes when the strands lie together.

attaching cones and clasp

❶ Gather the wires at one end of the necklace. Twist them together and trim to 1 in. (2.5cm) (**photo c**).

❷ On one end of a head pin or 3-in. (7.6cm) piece of 22-gauge wire, make a wrapped loop (see "Basics"). Put the twisted wires halfway through the loop, bend them in half, and twist (**photo d**).

❸ Pull the head pin through the large opening in the cone to hide the twisted wire ends (**photo e**).

❹ Make the first half of a wrapped loop with the wire that extends above the cone. (If the cone's small hole is larger than about ⅛ in./3mm, keep the loop from being pulled back into the cone by first stringing a bead slightly larger than the opening.) Slip one part of the clasp or a wire figure-8 (see "making the clasp" below) onto the loop, then complete the wrapped loop.

❺ Repeat these steps to finish the other end of the necklace.

making the clasp

My clasp consists of two wire figure-8s and a hook with a spiral embellishment (**photo f**).

❶ To make a figure-8, use roundnose pliers to turn a ¼-in. (6mm) loop at one end of the 18-gauge wire. Position the pliers about ¼ in. below that loop and make another loop in the opposite direction. Trim the excess wire. The cut ends should butt up against the center portion of the wire. Make a second figure-8.

❷ For the hook, turn a ⅛-in. loop at one end of the 18-gauge wire using roundnose pliers. Hold the loop with chainnose pliers and wind the wire tail around the loop 2½ times to form a flat spiral approximately ½ in. (1.3cm) in diameter.

❸ Allow the tail to extend ¼ in. beyond the spiral, then bend it back into a U-shape. Finish the hook by making a small loop at the wire's end.

❹ Hammer the wire pieces several times to flatten and strengthen them, if desired. ❍ – *Sue Ki Wilcox*

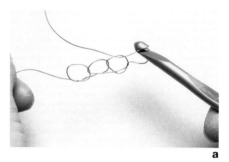

a

b

c

d

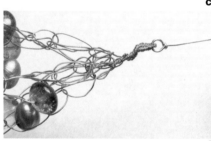

e

f

Braided crochet

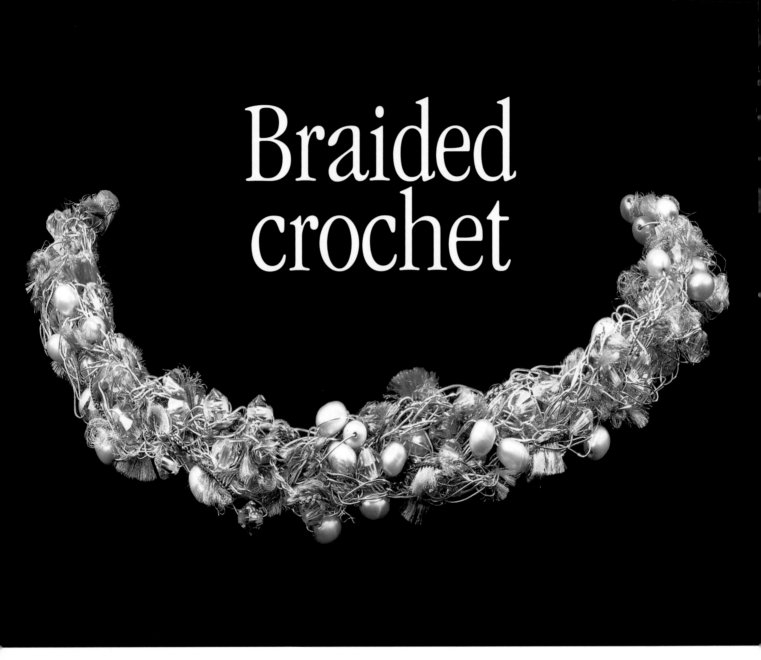

Lately, fashion magazines, clothing stores, and catalogs have been full of beautiful jewelry that is knitted or crocheted with beads. Wire and fancy yarns are also popular for adding textural dimension. This fun necklace combines these elements using only the simplest techniques.

To recreate this textured look, crochet nine chains of wire and beads and braid them together with fancy yarn. Conceal the ends of the braids with cones for a clean finish.

wire-crocheted chains

Wire doesn't slide once it's bent, so you can't easily tighten or loosen a stitch after it is made. Try to control the size of the loop before you begin the next stitch, but don't worry about any irregular stitches; they will blend in once the chains and strands of yarn are braided together.

❶ Randomly string pearls and crystals on the spool of 28-gauge wire. Don't cut the wire from the spool.

❷ Make the first chain stitch 3 in. (7.6cm) from the end of the wire (see

"Basics," p. 3). Crochet 2-3 medium-sized chain stitches.

❸ Slide a bead down to the hook and crochet a chain stitch (see "Basics" and **photo a**). Continue crocheting the chain and sliding beads down between random stitches.

Make the chain about one-third longer than the desired finished length of the necklace. The length of chain needed will depend on how tightly you braid the chains together. If the chains are too long, you can trim them later.

❹ Once the chain is the desired

length, cut the wire from the spool approximately 3 in. past the last stitch. Pull the tail through the last chain stitch to secure the chain.

5 Repeat steps 2-4 to make 9 beaded wire chains.

the first three braids

1 Carefully stretch the wire chains so the strands are more uniform. Cut a piece of yarn about 6 in. (15cm) longer than the chains. Hold 3 chains and the fiber in one hand and gently twist them together at one end (**photo b**).

2 Tape the twisted chains and fiber strand to your work surface or use T-pins to hold them on Foamcore. Separate the 3 chains and place the fiber strand over one of them (**photo c**).

3 Braid the 3 sections together. When you reach the bottom of the braid, twist the ends together as before.

4 Repeat steps 1-3 with the remaining 6 chains for a total of 3 braids.

necklace construction

1 Twist the 3 braids together at one end. Secure the twisted end to your work surface and braid the 3 braided sections together (**photo d**). Test-fit or measure the braid. If necessary, trim the braid to the desired length, leaving 3-in. tails. End by twisting the ends together as before.

2 Cut a 5-in. (13cm) length of 20-gauge wire and wrap it around one twisted end of the braided chains a few times (**photo e**).

3 Trim the end of the braid to about ¼ in. (6mm) past the wire wrap. Fold the trimmed end down next to the wrap and continue wrapping the wire, leaving about a 3-in. tail (**photo f**). Use chainnose pliers to squeeze the 20-gauge wire around the braided ends.

4 Slide a cone on the wire and push it over the wire-wrapped end. String a bead on the wire. (If the cone has a large hole, string a 4mm round silver bead between the cone and the bead.) Make the first half of a wrapped loop (see "Basics").

5 Slide one clasp part into the loop (**photo g**). Finish the wrap and trim the excess wire.

6 Repeat steps 1-5 on the other end of the necklace. **○** – *Gloria Farver*

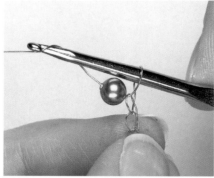

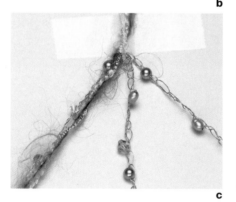

materials
- **1** Spool 28-gauge wire
- **10 in.** (25cm) 20-gauge Wire
- **200-325** 4-6mm Assorted pearls and Austrian crystals or glass beads
- **2** 4mm Round silver beads (optional)
- **2** Cones
- **3-5 yd.** (2.7-4.5m) Fancy yarn
- **1** Clasp
- Crochet hook, size 7

Tools: chain- and roundnose pliers, wire cutters; Foamcore and T-pins (optional)

Beaded purse

the thread in the direction of the twist to make it tighter and thinner. Continue twisting until the polish is evenly distributed and nearly dry. When it's dry, add a second and possibly a third coat if the thread isn't stiff enough. Cut the end off at a taper to produce a needlelike point.

2 For the first side of the purse, string 5 strands of beads (about 1,000), being careful to keep the thread from snarling. You'll need to keep about 2 yd. (1.8m) of thread and some beads available to work with, and you'll keep pushing the rest of the beads toward the ball as you use the thread.

3 Begin with the knobless start (**figure 1**) and chain 2. The loop formed in the knobless start is the first chain; leave it fairly large with a long tail (3-4 in. / 7.6-10cm) and let it turn so you can work over the tail (**figure 2**).

4 Hold the tail against the loop and work 6 bead stitches in the loop and over the tail. To work a bead stitch, push a bead up and work a single crochet (yarn over the hook and pull a loop through the loop into which the hook is inserted (**photo a**). Yarn over the hook and pull through both loops on the hook (**photo b**).

5 Pull the tail to close the loop partway but not yet tightly. Place a piece of contrast thread over the work (the row marker) so that it will rest between the last stitch (st) of the first round and the first stitch of the second round.

Round 2: Work 2 bead single crochet (bds) in each st (12 sts). To work bds, push up a bead, insert the hook in the back loop of the stitch below, yarn over (**photo c**), and pull through the loop. Yarn over and pull through both loops. At the end of each round, flip the long end of the marking thread over the work and continue (**photo d**).

Round 3: Work 2 bds in the first st and 1 bds in the second. Continue around in this manner (18 sts).

Round 4: Work 1 bds in the first st, *2 bds in the next st, 1 bds in the next 2 sts*. Repeat from * to * to the end of the round, ending with 1 bds (24 sts).

Round 5: 2 bds in the first st *1 bds in the next 3 sts, 2 bds in the next st*. Repeat from * to * around, ending with 1 bds in each of the last three sts (30 sts).

D iscus, the purse shown here, is much easier to make than it looks. Each side is a single-crochet beaded spiral, and it closes securely with a snap fastener. It's just the right size for an evening bag or a necessities purse that you can carry inside a larger handbag.

Stitch size should equal bead size so the work will lie flat. Transfer beads to the crochet cotton for one side of the purse at a time. Discard any misshapen beads. After crocheting both sides of the purse, join them and make the strap with the thread from the second piece.

purse sides
1 The crochet cotton completely fills the beads, so you can't use a needle to thread them. Instead, stiffen the last 2 in. (5cm) of thread with clear nail polish. While the polish is drying, twist

Round 6: 1 bds in the first 2 sts *2 bds in the next st, 1 bds in the next 4 sts*. Repeat from * to *; end 1 bds in the last 2 sts (36 sts).

Round 7: 2 bds in the first st *1 bds in the next 5 sts, 2 bds in the next st*. Repeat from * to *, ending with 1 bds in each of the last 5 sts (42 sts).

Most of the beads in round 1 will be on the right side. Thread the starting tail in the tapestry needle and, after pushing all the beads to the beaded side, tighten the beginning loop (**photo e**). Run the starting thread through several stitches on the wrong side and fasten it off.

Round 8: 1 bds in the first 3 sts *2 bds in the next st, 1 bds in the next 6 sts*. Repeat from * to *, ending with 1 bds in the last 3 sts (48 sts).

Round 9: 2 bds in the first st *1 bds in the next 7 sts, 2 bds in the next st*. Repeat from * to *, ending with 1 bds in each of the last 7 sts (54 sts).

Round 10: 1 bds in the first 4 sts *2 bds in the next st, 1 bds in the next 8 sts*. Repeat from * to *, ending with 1 bds in the last 4 sts (60 sts).

Round 11: 2 bds in the first st *1 bds in the next 9 sts, 2 bds in the next st*. Repeat from * to *, ending with 1 bds in the last 9 sts (66 sts).

Round 12: 1 bds in the first 5 sts *2 bds in the next st, 1 bds in the next 10 sts*. Repeat from * to *, ending with 1 bds in the last 5 sts (72 sts).

Round 13: 2 bds in the first st *1 bds in the next 11 sts, 2 bds in the next st*. Repeat from * to *, ending with 1 bds in the last 11 sts (78 sts).

Round 14: 1 bds in the first 6 sts *2 bds in the next st, 1 bds in the next 12 sts*. Repeat from * to *, ending with 1 bds in the last 6 sts (84 sts).

Round 15: 2 bds in the first st *1 bds in the next 13 sts, 2 bds in the next st*. Repeat from * to *, ending with 1 bds in the last 13 sts (90 sts).

Round 16: 1 bds in the first 7 sts *2 bds in the next st, 1 bds in the next 14 sts*. Repeat from * to *, ending with 1 bds in the last 7 sts (96 sts).

Round 17: Work even (96 bds). At the end of the round, push up a bead and slip stitch (bd sl st) in the first st of the round. (To bd sl st, push up a bead, hook through the next stitch, yarn over, and pull the yarn through the

a

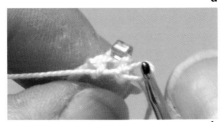

b

c

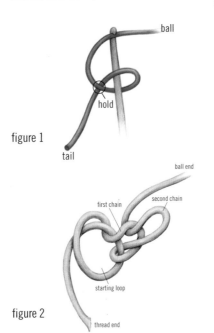

d

e

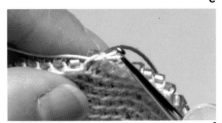

f

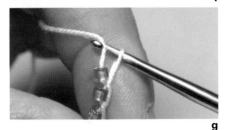

g

h

i

ball

hold

figure 1

tail

ball end

first chain   second chain

starting loop

figure 2

thread end

stitch and the loop on the hook—see "Basics" and **photo f**). Leave a tail to weave in and pull it through the last stitch to end. Remove the marker thread.

❻ Before working the second piece, loosely chain (ch) 8 beads (**photo g**), leaving long tails (about 6-8 in. / 15-20cm) at each end. You'll attach this later to the rest of the strap (see "finishing steps," step 4).

❼ Transfer the rest of the hank of beads to the thread and work the second piece as for the first through round 17, but DO NOT end the thread.

finishing steps

❶ To make a tasseled, beaded cord, use the same thread and start against the last stitch of round 17. Loosely ch 72 beads. Push up 30 beads and slip stitch (no bead) into the last ch. Repeat to make five 30-bead loops (**photo h**).

❷ Working through the top or back loop of the bead chain, loosely bd sl st in each bd ch back to the beginning.

❸ Continuing with the same thread right against the last stitch, hold the two sides together with the beads facing outward. Work through the sl st of both pieces. Then bd sl st in the next 66 pairs of stitches (**photo i**).

❹ To make the strap, continue with the same thread right against the beadwork and loosely bd ch 124 sts. Pick up the 8-bd ch piece from step 6 of "purse sides" and bd sl st through its back loops. Wrap the short piece around the tasseled cord (this makes the strap adjustable) and weave in the ends with the tapestry needle. Bd sl st back to the start of the strap. End the work. Then thread the tails on the tapestry needle and weave them in neatly.

❺ Sew a snap to the middle of the opening. ● – *Dana Kahan Benjamin*

materials

- • 1 Ball DMC Cebelia crochet cotton, size 10
- • 1 Hank 8º seed beads, 2-cut, or hex-cut
- • #3 or 4 Steel crochet hook
- • 12-18 in. (30-46cm) Thread scrap in contrasting color
- • #22 Tapestry needle
- • Clear nail polish
- • Snap set, optional

Beaded handbag

Crocheted bags are the rage these days. You see them everywhere, from Hollywood to New York City to your local college campus. Add beads to your crocheted bag for extra pizazz. This versatile purse, inspired by vintage photos of women with parasols and beaded handbags, can be either dressy or casual, based on the beads you choose. It's easy to make using a few basic crochet stitches, but if you're not familiar with them, read through the instructions before beginning and practice those that are new to you.

handbag base

❶ Chain-stitch (ch) a base row 3½-in. (8.8cm) long (see "Basics," p. 3).

❷ Work a single crochet (sc) (see "Basics") in each ch until you reach the end. Work 3 sc in the end stitch (do not turn). Keeping the base flat, rotate to work sc in each stitch on the other side of the chain. Work 3 sc in the end stitch. (On subsequent rounds, the "end" is the second stitch of each 3sc cluster worked on the previous round. Each round has 2 ends.)

❸ Repeat step 2 four times.

❹ *Sc in the next 4 stitches. Work 2 sc in the fifth stitch. Sc until you reach the fifth stitch from the end. Work 2 sc in the fifth stitch. Sc to the end. Work 3 sc in the end stitch.* Repeat from * to * on the other side of the oval.

❺ Alternate between steps 2 and 4 until the piece measures approximately 6½ x 3 in. (16.3 x 7.6cm) or the size you prefer.

❻ To make the picot detail on the bottom edge, *sc in the next 3 stitches, working into the outside loop only, ch 3.* Repeat from * to * around the base.

❼ Sc in each stitch around the base, working into the inside loop only.

❽ Sc in each stitch around the base for the next 3 rounds.

❾ Cut the cord, leaving a long tail to weave in later. To block, or shape, the base, pin it down tightly so it lies flat, moisten thoroughly, and let it dry overnight.

beaded body

❶ Thread a Big-Eye needle with the crochet cord. String 3-4 ft. (.9-1.2m) of beads. Tie the cord to the tail against

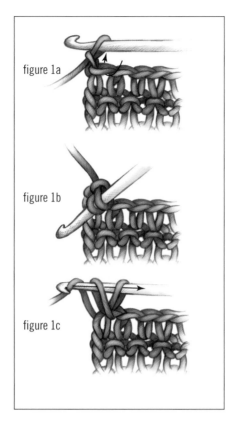

figure 1a

figure 1b

figure 1c

the edge of the base with a square knot (see "Basics").

❷ Alternate 1 sc and 1 bead single crochet (bd sc) (see "Basics") around the base. Continue until the bag's sides measure 6-7 in. (15-18cm). String more beads as needed.

❸ Working without beads, *sc in the next 11 stitches and decrease in the 12th stitch.* Repeat from * to * for the next 4 rounds.

To decrease, enter the 12th stitch as for an sc, take the cord over the hook, and pull the loop through the stitch only, leaving 2 loops on the hook. Repeat in the 13th stitch. Yarn over again and pull through all 3 loops.

drawstring and ruffle

❶ To create the open spaces for the drawstring, ch 5, *skip 1 sc, double crochet (dc) (see "Basics") in the next stitch, ch 1.* Repeat from * to *. When you return to the ch 5, slip stitch into the third ch. (To slip stitch, insert the hook through the chain, bring the yarn over the hook, and pull the hook back through the chain and loop— see "Basics.")

❷ Start the ruffle. *Make 2 sc in the space created by the ch 1, above, and

materials

• **2-3** Balls Opera crochet cotton, #5
• 120g Seed beads, size 8º or 8º hex cuts
• Crochet hook, size C
• Big Eye needle
• Tapestry needle
• 48-in. (1.2m) Decorative cord for drawstring (available in fabric stores)

2 sc in the dc.* Repeat from * to * to the end of the round.

❸ *Work 1 sc in the first sc then 2 sc in the next sc.* Repeat from * to * to the end of the round.

❹ Work 1 sc in each sc for the next 4 rounds. Weave in the tails.

strap

❶ String 3-4 ft. of beads on the cord.

❷ Working without beads, ch 8, turn, skip the first ch, and sc back to the start (7 sc). Work in sc for 2½ in. (6.3cm).

❸ Ch 1. Alternate 1 sc and 1 bd sc three times, ending with an sc. Turn, ch 1, and work the next row in sc. Repeat these 2 rows until the strap measures 41 in. (1.02m). End with 2½ in. (6.3cm) of sc.

❹ To finish the edge around the strap, work in sc along all four sides. Work a second round in crab stitch (reverse single crochet). For crab stitch, with the work at your right, enter the first stitch on the right, yarn over, and pull through. Yarn over and pull through both loops (**figures 1a-c**).

❺ Tie off the cord, weave in the tail, and block the strap.

finishing

❶ Lay the bag on a flat surface. Place the strap's ends inside at each side of the bag. Align the strap's end rows of beads with the drawstring loops. Make sure the beads face outward.

❷ Thread a tapestry needle with cord and sew the strap ends onto the wrong side of the bag. Sew along the sc edging and across a row of sc (below the beadwork). Make sure your stitches aren't visible on the surface.

❸ Weave a drawstring through the open spaces below the ruffle, starting and ending in the center of one of the sides. Embellish the drawstring's ends with beads. ● – *Linda Lehman*

Filigree bracelets

These lacy bracelets are real attention-getters. Although you can make them with conventional materials, like sterling silver, gold-filled, and copper wire, try making the bracelets with colorful craft wires instead.

If you know how to crochet, you can easily complete a bracelet in an evening. Beginners will need to learn a few basic stitches before getting started. The fun part is getting to play with the endless variations of beads and wire.

When you crochet with wire, it's important to control the size of the loop before you begin the next stitch. With fibers, you can usually adjust the tension after a stitch is complete. But wire doesn't slide once it's bent, so you can't easily tighten or loosen your stitches after they are made. Fortunately, any irregularity in the stitches adds to the overall laciness of the design.

❶ Transfer approximately 85 beads to the spool of wire.

❷ Chain stitch (ch) (see "Basics," p. 3) a strip that is 1½ in. (4cm) longer than your wrist measurement and has an even number of stitches. (The gauge for these bracelets is flexible, but most of mine have 6-7 stitches per in./2.5cm. Try to match the stitch size to the beads you're using.) Straighten out the chain.

Row 1: Turn and work a single crochet (sc) (see "Basics") in the second ch from the hook. Slide a bead into place against the sc and make a bead single crochet (bds) (see "Basics") in the next ch. Alternate between sc and bds across the row. End with an sc (**photo a**).

Row 2: Turn, ch 3, and double crochet (dc) (see "Basics") in the first sc (it has no bead) (**photo b**). *Slide a bead against the loop on the hook and make a bead chain stitch (bd ch) (see "Basics"). Dc in the next sc (no bead).* Repeat from * to * across the row.

Row 3: Turn, ch 3, and dc in the first dc. *Make 1 bd ch and dc in the next dc.* Repeat from * to * across the row.

Row 4: Repeat row 3.

Row 5: Turn, ch 1, and sc in each stitch across the row.

❸ Instead of turning, as in previous rows, sc to the midpoint of the narrow end. To make the clasp loop, work

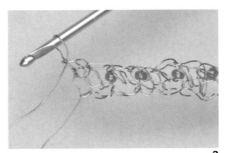

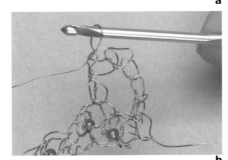

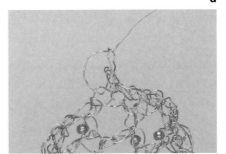

approximately 12-14 ch to go over your closure bead. Slip stitch (sl st) (see "Basics") around the loop to reinforce it (**photo c**).

Continue in sc to finish the narrow end. You'll be at the bracelet's starting point. Twist the working wire and tail together (**photo d**), then trim them to about ½ in. (1.3cm). Use pliers to coil the wires tightly, flatten the coil, and hide it on the wrong side of the bracelet.

❹ Cut a 1-ft. (30cm) length of wire and secure it to either corner of the other narrow end. Sc to the middle of this edge, as above. Remove the hook and pull the wire through the loop to knot it (**photo e**).

String the clasp bead and a smaller bead and go back through the clasp bead. Wrap the wire around the base of the clasp bead, go through the beads again to reinforce them, then wind the wire around the base several times to form a shank (**photo f**).

❺ Insert the hook into the next stitch along the edge, pull a loop of wire through the stitch and continue

materials

- **1** 30-yd. (27m) Spool 28-gauge wire
- **80-90** Glass, sterling silver, or gold-filled beads, any size from 8º to 6mm
- **1** 10-14mm Bead for clasp
- Steel crochet hook, size 2

Tools: chainnose pliers, wire cutters

working in sc to finish this edge. Pull the wire through the loop and weave the tail into the bracelet to hide the end. Trim the excess wire.

❻ Gently push the beads to the front. ◗

– Deanne A. Nanna

Beaded totem doll

This beaded doll is a fun way to combine beads with traditional crochet or bead crochet. Use a small disk mirror for the face and decorate your doll in whatever colors and designs appeal to you. You may be surprised at the deep meanings people find in your doll.

The bodies of these beautiful little figures are crocheted and then decorated with glass beads. A pattern of the basic doll shape is included if you prefer a sewn cloth doll (**figure 1**). Enlarge the pattern on a photocopier and add seam allowances when you cut out the fabric.

For the crocheted doll, construct two round head pieces, one built around a mirror, and crochet them together around the sides and top. Then crochet the two body pieces and join them. After stuffing the head and body firmly, sew them together at the neck. For a cloth doll, blanket stitch around the mirror to hold it on. Sew the front and back together, right sides facing, leaving one side open to turn the doll through. Stuff; then blindstitch the side closed.

Now comes the fun: decorate your doll with beads.

crochet a doll

Head *Row 1:* Chain (ch) 3 (see "Basics," p. 3), double crochet (dc) 12 (see "Basics,") in the third ch from hook, join to form a circle. Ch 2 (do not turn).

Row 2: 2 half double crochet (hdc) (see "Basics") in each dc stitch around —24 hdc—join, ch 1.

Row 3: Single crochet (sc) (see "Basics") in each hdc around—24 sc— join, ch 1.

Row 4: *1 sc in each of the next 2 sc stitches, skip the next sc, 1 sc over the next sc.* Continue around from * to *, easing in the mirror disk (**photo a**)— 18 sc—join.

Row 5: 1 slip stitch (sl st) (see "Basics") in each sc around. Cut the thread and pull through the last loop.
Other side of the head Repeat rows 1-3.

Row 4: Sc in each sc, at the same time catching the loop from row 4 of the mirror disk side (mirror disk out) for 18 stitches. Six skipped stitches on the mirror disk base and the head back (12 total) remain open for the neck. Cut the thread and pull through the last loop.
Body (make 2)—*Row 1:* Ch 28. Sc in the second ch from the hook and in each ch across—27 sc. Ch 1 and turn at the end of each row.

Row 2: Sc in each sc across—27 sc.

Rows 3-4: Repeat row 2 (4 rows of 27 sc for the arms).

Row 5: Sl st across 8 sc, ch 1, sc across 11 stitches.

Row 6: Sc across 11 stitches.

Rows 7-16: Repeat row 6 (12 rows of 11 sc for the body).

Row 17: Sc across 5 stitches.

Rows 18-25: Repeat row 17 (9 rows of 5 sc for a leg). Cut the thread and pull through the last loop.
Other leg Attach the thread to the 7th sc of the lower body; repeat rows 17-25.
Finishing Sc evenly all the way around each doll body piece without turning. Then sc or sew the front and back of the body together, leaving the neck open. Stuff the body and head. Then sew the head onto the neck opening.

beading the doll

Let your imagination be your guide as you decorate your doll. Choose hot, bright colors or soft pastels or go monochromatic. Then use bead embroidery stitches and your favorite off-loom techniques to clothe your doll. Cover the figure with personal symbols or dress her realistically. You may be surprised at how she turns out.

For the lavender doll (front above and back at left), I strung seed beads on the yarn before crocheting and added them on many of the yarn overs as I crocheted the base (see "Basics" for bead single crochet). You can produce a similar effect by sewing beads on after the doll is stuffed. **Photo b** shows

figure 1
(half size)

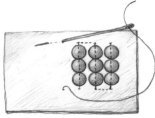

figure 2

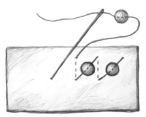

figure 3

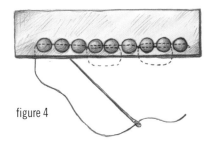

figure 4

a

b

c

d

e

applying them to the body with half-cross stitch, which you may know from needlepoint as tent stitch. Bring the thread up in one corner of the stitch, string a bead, and sew down in the diagonally opposite corner (**figure 2**).

Use lane stich for the arm bands and seed bead/bugle collar. To do lane stitch, bring the needle up at the start of a lane (line), string 3-5 beads (no more), and go down so the lane is perfectly vertical. Take a horizontal half-bead-wide stitch on the back and come up next to where you went down. String the 3-5 bead pattern and go down next to the start of the first lane (**photo c** and **figure 3**). Keep lanes straight and even.

Use backstitch bead appliqué for outlining appliqué motifs or making lines or circles. Bring the needle up at the beginning of the line, *string 3 beads, and go down right against the third bead. Bring the needle back up between the first 2 beads strung and go through beads 2 and 3 again. Repeat from * (**photo d** and **figure 4**). To smooth lines and circles after adding all the beads, run the thread through the beads again. Fill in outlines with interesting beads or beads backstitched on one at a time.

I also like to tack on a skirt (**photo e**) made with square stitch or peyote stitch (see "Basics"). To add fringe dangles to the bottom of the skirt, exit through the bottom hole of any bead at the hem of the skirt and add three or more seed or bugle beads. Sew back through all the beads but the one on the very end. Repeat this on as many of the edge beads as you wish to create either a full or simple fringe. ☉
– *Pat Chiovarie with Kathlyn Moss*

materials

- 1-in. (2.5cm) Round mirror (crafts store)
- **3** Skeins pearl cotton #5
- #5 (1.9mm) Steel crochet hook (#4 if you crochet loosely)
- Fiber fill
- #12 Sharps or beading needle
- Nymo B beading thread
- Variety of glass beads: 11º, 8º, and 6º seed beads, 3mm bugles, 4-6mm semi-precious stone beads, charms, etc.

Bead ropes

Crocheted bead ropes are beautiful but they often stretch badly. In addition, the ends often look clunky with the beads going in a different direction. My technique will solve both problems.

After stringing the beads, make the bead rope in a two-step process. The first time around you put on the beads, and the next time around you lock the beads of the previous round into place as you put on the beads for the next round. Start with a bracelet and alternate two colors or a stripe and a solid so you can keep count easily.

starting the tube

❶ Thread all the beads on the cord, alternating stripe and solid. Leave the ball attached to the cord.

❷ To start, make 6 medium-sized chain stitches (see "Basics," p. 3), leaving an 8-in. (20cm) tail. Join the end to the beginning with a slip stitch (sl st) (see "Basics" and **photo a**).

❸ Go through two loops of the first stitch from the inside of the circle with the hook tip facing out away from you.

❹ Slide the first bead (solid) down to the circle and hold it in place with your middle finger. Catch the thread on the other side of the bead (**photo b**) and pull it through the stitch and the loop. This is a slip stitch; one loop remains.

❺ Go through the next stitch and slip the striped bead down to the circle. Catch the thread and pull it through the stitch and the loop on the hook. One loop remains.

❻ After adding the 5th bead, you'll be back at the tail. Go through the stitch just left of the tail (right for lefties) to add the 6th bead (**photo c**). Notice how the beads fan out around the circle. They won't form a neat tube until the third row.

❼ You are at what I call the "curb," which is the starting place for the second row. This is where you are most likely to lose a stitch, but after you've passed it 2-3 times, it won't be there anymore to confuse you.

❽ To begin row 2, insert the hook to the left (right for lefties) of the solid bead (**photo d**). Push the new bead up between the last and first beads of row 1. The thread may want to loop under the first bead. Don't let it! It must loop above the first bead of the first row (**photo e**) or the beads won't sit straight with their holes vertical. Pull the thread through both loops. This step is the key to the entire technique.

❾ Bead 2 is a stripe and should sit above and slightly to the left (right) of the stripe below. As you insert the hook from inside to outside and to the left (right) of the stripe below, hold the thread out at a 45° angle to the hook so it won't loop under the old bead. Slide the new bead in place and pull the thread through both loops.

crocheting the tube

❶ After row 3, the beadwork will have formed an obvious tube and the curb will be gone. As you continue working, the bead colors will spiral like a candy cane. A little thread will show at first, but keep working snugly, and it will soon disappear.

❷ When you've worked 4-5 rounds, stick the butt end of your hook into the tube to widen it and thread the nylon core cord through. This cord keeps the rope from stretching indefinitely after the project is finished. Insert the cord when the rope is short. Tie a safety pin on each end or a cluster of 3 beads so it won't pull through the tube. Continue bead-crocheting around the core (**photo f**) until the bracelet plus the center bead is about 1½ in. (3.8cm) longer than your wrist measurement. End with a round of sl st without beads to align the last bead row correctly.

❸ If your start was messy, you can fix it before joining the ends of the bracelet. Here's how: Carefully cut off the starting chain. Pull up the first bead. Then pull out the inside part of the loop, the part that's closer to the next bead. Continue removing beads this way until you've removed the messy row(s) and have a tail that's at least 6-8 in. (15-20cm) long. As you look down on the tube end, each bead will seem to be attached to the tube center by a single line (spoke) of thread. To align the first row properly, you need to crochet a sl st under each spoke in the opposite direction to your work (**photo g**). Sl st once more under the first spoke, then pull the thread through the loop to secure it.

finishing the bracelet

❶ String the centerpiece bead onto one end of the core cord.

❷ With your hand folded as narrowly as possible (tuck the thumb under the middle fingers), tie or have a friend tie the core cord ends around the widest part of your hand with a surgeon's knot (see "Basics"). Be sure the knot is secure. The core cord will be ½ to 1½ in. (1.3-3.8cm) longer than the crocheted rope, but you'll close this gap beginning in step 4, below. This core limits how much the bracelet can stretch, preventing it from getting so loose it falls off your wrist.

❸ Use the butt end of the hook to open one end of the tube and pull the knot inside to bury it. Trim the tails.

❹ Thread one perle cotton tail onto a #10 tapestry needle and go under the chain row (the crown) from the inside to the outside. Go through the centerpiece bead. Then go under the crown opposite the tail from outside to inside and go back through the bead.

❺ Go under the crown on the starting side from outside to inside opposite the first stitch. Finally go through the bead and sew from outside to inside under the crown next to the other tail (**photo h**).

❻ Now jiggle the beadwork until the thread is snug and tie the tails together with a square knot (see "Basics").

❼ Use the threaded tail to pull in any thread showing on the crowns. End this thread by going back through the rope. Take a small backstitch around a rope thread, go through more of the rope and repeat. Backstitch the other tail into the rope. Do not sew through any beads.

clasped necklace with centerpiece

Make two crocheted rope sections. To determine the length of each section, subtract the length of the centerpiece bead and clasp from the desired length of the necklace and divide by 2.

❶ After completing the first rope piece around a long, doubled core cord, string the centerpiece bead on the core cord. Then crochet the second rope around the core cord. Join the ropes through the centerpiece bead as you did in "finishing the bracelet," steps 4-7. Bury the cotton tails at the clasp ends, too.

❷ Thread both core cords at one end through a bead cap from inside to outside, go through the clasp ring, and come back through the cap.

❸ Tie the core ends in a square knot on one side of the core strand, turn the work over and tie another square knot on the other side of the strand. Repeat on the first side again. Seal the knot with G-S Hypo Cement. When dry, feed the core strands back into the crocheted tube.

❹ Repeat steps 2-3 on the other end of the necklace, pulling the core strand tight before knotting (**photo i**). ●

– *Nicolette Stessin*

materials

- #7 or 6 Steel crochet hook, Clover hook #2
- #7 Suture needle, #10 tapestry needle, or twisted wire needle
- 2 Small safety pins or leftover beads

bracelet
- 30-35g (1-1¼ oz.) 6º Seed beads (half striped, half solid or 2 colors)
- 1 Ball or skein #5 DMC perle cotton or equivalent to match beads
- 1 Centerpiece bead (2mm or larger hole)
- 36 in. (.9m) Nylon bead cord #3 or larger

necklace with clasp
- 75-80g (3 oz.) 6º Seed beads 1-2 colors
- 1 Ball #5 DMC perle cotton to match beads
- 1 Centerpiece bead (2mm or larger hole)
- 2 yd. (1.8m) Nylon bead cord #3 or larger
- 2 Bead caps, 10-12mm diameter
- 1 Clasp with 2 soldered rings or split rings
- G-S Hypo Cement

a

d

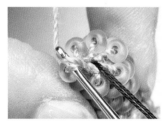

g

b

e

h

c

f

i

Get Great Jewelry Projects All Through the Year!

Your Beading Resource!

Bead&Button magazine

- New and traditional stitching techniques
- Fully-tested projects
- Step-by-step instructions and photos

BeadStyle magazine

- Beautiful pieces in today's hottest styles
- Make jewelry in an evening or less
- Great photos and easy-to-follow instructions

If you enjoyed *Bead Crochet*, make sure you order these titles from the Easy-Does-It Series.

Subscribe or Order Today and Enjoy
New Beading Projects Every Month!

Call 1-800-533-6644 or visit
beadandbuttonbooks.com

KALMBACH
PUBLISHING CO.

ISBN 978-0-89024-448-7 $7.95 U.S. 12272